THE STENCH
*
POEMS

*
JABULANI MZINYATHI

Mwanaka Media and Publishing Pvt Ltd,
Chitungwiza Zimbabwe
*
Creativity, Wisdom and Beauty

Publisher: *Mmap*
Mwanaka Media and Publishing Pvt Ltd
24 Svosve Road, Zengeza 1
Chitungwiza Zimbabwe
mwanaka@yahoo.com
mwanaka13@gmail.com
www.africanbookscollective.com/publishers/mwanaka-media-and-publishing
https://facebook.com/MwanakaMediaAndPublishing/

Distributed in and outside N. America by African Books Collective
orders@africanbookscollective.com
www.africanbookscollective.com

ISBN: 978-1-77928-411-2
EAN: 9781779284112

© Jabulani Mzinyathi 2025

All rights reserved.
No part of this book may be reproduced or transmitted in any form or by any means, mechanical or electronic, including photocopying and recording, or be stored in any information storage or retrieval system, without written permission from the publisher

DISCLAIMER
All views expressed in this publication are those of the author and do not necessarily reflect the views of *Mmap*.

Dedication
This work is dedicated to all the emasculated people living in abject poverty. This work owes its existence in part to Frantz Fanon and Ngugi wa Thiong'o. Black Skin, White Masks and Moving The Centre were ' sound tracks' as I worked on this ' reality show.'

Acknowledgements

I am eternally grateful to my wife, children and grandchildren. They have to accept that I work late at night after grappling with issues to do with my profession as a lawyer. It is not an easy road as Buju Banton, Jamaican reggae artist says. I am eternally grateful to my publisher for giving me another opportunity to come up with this collection. I am eternally grateful to fellow poets in the *Zimbolicious* and *Best "New" African Poets* stables.

CONTENTS

Part Of The Legacy
Second Routing
Trinkets
The Investors
Gang Raped
Getting A Beating
Self Preservation
Tongue Lashing
THE STENCH
Friends Or Fiends
Friendly Fire In Zimbabwe
Souls For Sale
Statuette Silence
The *Chitutes*
The Unthinkable
Listening
Anomie
Where Are They?
Terrible Twins
Daggers Sharpened
Burial Ground
Gweru
Littered Road
Done And Dusted
A Fool's Sordid Tale
Sold Souls
The Donkey
What Happened?
Symptoms
Of Blindness And Darkness
Not A Justification

The Fairy Tale
Off The Hook
One Way Ticket
The Monstrosity
Summing Up
Their Ways
Reflections
The Grave Digger
The Nocturnal Announcement
Pyrrhus
Vultures
Thought Police
Saints
Weird World
The Broth
Winter Be Gone
Forever Changing
A New Morality
The End
Recess
Of Blips And Blunders
Saka Muchaita Sei? (What will you do?)
The Beginning Of The End
The Patriots
The Influences
Stolen
Dry Pool
Quaking
Crumbs
Evil Inheritance
The Way It Is
Now
Invoking Spirits

Tramp
Thick Mist
Pests
The Shitstem
Vhembe
In This Mind
Slaves
School Boys
Deep Chasms
Alms
Vampire
Beggars
Nothing
Skewed
The Symbols
Feeding Trough Aspirant
Baying For His Blood
My Ant Voice
Triple K Man
Same Old Song

Introductory note by the poet

This collection is made up of poems dealing with putrefaction. There is a pungent or acrid smell. It is emanating from the corruption that pervades Zimbabwe. That is no secret at all.
The stench stems from the activities of some of the so-called investors who leave us with holes in the ground and poisonous substances like mercury and cyanide. There is a looming catastrophe if we sit on our laurels and do nothing about it.
The acrid smell is stemming from the rampant drug abuse that is bedeviling our society. Mental health issues abound in Zimbabwe.
The pungent smell is also from the mounds of poverty. It is also from the obscene riches and warped philanthropy. Joseph Hil of the Jamaican reggae group Culture sang, ' Mr Richman share the riches with the poor before they share the poverty with you.' The poor will feed on the rich. Time is nigh for enlightened self-interest. This concept means that one looks after themselves by taking care of others.
There is the foul smell of political bickering, jostling for the feeding trough, entitlement, self-preservation and self-glorification. Statues erected today may be demolished tomorrow. History has many such examples. Self-exaltation cannot last forever.
There is putrefaction emanating from the culture of begging for cars and other trinkets. The moral compass has been lost. This poet is asking for serious introspection and the return to values that have stood the test of time.
The collection also has poems of an autobiographical nature about the foul smell of sordid affairs. That too is the stench at the personal level.
There is also the foul smell that is emanating from the international scene. The hyacinth of American economic and possibly military adventurism is threatening the livelihoods of many across the globe.

Donald Trump is on a war path. African unity remains an unattainable ideal due to capitulation by some countries to the tariffs hogwash propagated by the American system that has no respect for Africa.

In terms of language use one will easily notice that there has been use of some chiShona words and isiNdebele/ isiZulu words. Readers are advised to get translations on their own in some cases. The experience is quite enriching. There is also a sprinkling of patois in one or two of the poems. The world we are living in requires some versatility and an understanding of current trends.

Part Of The Legacy

You were on your ego trip
Obsessed with amassing power
Later you were on a dynasty path
We know it later turned nasty

You left a tattered and torn nation
Chibwechitedza's plans you derailed
All talk of nationalism was a mask
Just a mask for archaic tribal hegemony

Tomorrow's intellectuals mired in it
With tenacity holding on to your ways
Spreading crazy tribal superiority ideas
Another part of your disease laden legacy

Second Routing

They had to ward off
Ward off tropical diseases
They then subjugated us
With the bible, bullet and gun
In language, dress...we aped them

In come their friends from the east
Invited for so-called mega deals
Just a euphemism for enslavement
Our natural resources going for a song
The unemployed driven into slavery
Nothing to show but just a pittance

Operating under shrouds of secrecy
The owners of the wealth dehumanized
Sold by the elite that gets the gains
Nagasaki and Hiroshima will be child's play
When the potency of the poison sets on

Trinkets

Just for a few bloody trinkets
Many you sell into this slavery
Hear the wailing of our people
While you show off your wheels
Obtained from the broken backs
Of the bawling oppressed masses

Your smile like the morning rising sun
You receive that cursed blood money
They have you under closed circuit TV
Your villainy was long put on record
Now you take the side of these creatures
No crumbs fall from their high tables

The Investors

Not with shackles and chains
No longer going across the seas
Dead bodies not thrown to sharks
Right here on the African continent
Joseph still sold by his brother's
Yesterday it was the white or pink man
Today the slit eyed heartless yellow man
Call it xenophobia but this is that indignation
That righteous indignation against evil
All that is remaining are the poisoned rivers
The cyanide and mercury poisoned streams
All we are left with are death laden wells
Our brothers and sisters sell us into slavery
With their concubines in tow of they fly
Off to France, Malaysia, Dubai just for leisure
Off they fly to China, India and Singapore
Leaving us to die of curable, multiple diseases
We are being sold for them to be in mansions
While we are drowning in seas of poverty
All they do is flaunt shameless profligacy

Gang Raped

Yesterday it was the white man
Perhaps more pink than white
Against those more brown than black
Not anger but righteous indignation
The raping of our land then started
Today the gang raping continues
The yellow man ravishing the land
Aided and abetted by the sons of the soil
Parting her legs for the yellow phallus to drill
Everywhere the poisons polluting
The mountains, hills and valleys blasted
Clueless rulers getting just the crumbs
The wealth siphoned by their friends
Their so-called friends from the east
There where thick wintry darkness rises
While the devils rub their hands in glee
Ready to receive just worthless peanuts
Putrid and insipid ideas ruin the future
Nothing to inherit but poisoned water sources
Nothing to inherit but mercury poisoning
Nothing to inherit but cyanide poisoning

Getting A Beating

Mother nature wields her whip
Her errant children must be chastised
She has been stripped of her clothes
Rivers have been swallowed by silt
Her suicidal children still disobedient
Ozone layer depleting gases abound
Temperatures rising to shocking levels
Water tables now forever receding
The so-called progress is just suicide
With no trace of sustainable development
Dennis Brutus saw planet polluting greed

Self Preservation

The inevitable is happening
The old giving way to the new
Look there goes the setting sun
The sun will rise again in the east
There is a blood bath in the east
Look who is fingered for meddling
To the north the routing took place
The middle finger was long shown
The meddling in the west bore no fruit
Voices of protest in the south west
The deep desire for self preservation
The chocking isolation is fast taking root
The sale by date has long come and gone

Tongue Lashing

Mara why ANC
Why why Ramaphosa
How could you lose it
Lose it to those upstarts
You want to bring back apartheid
Now we believe what that boy said
That you never were in the trenches
That you were just *impimpi*
That opportunity who captured Mandela
How could *umdala* upstage you
Why did you not play the race card
Here we have used it successfully before
Kanti have you not heard of nikuv
With the state resources at your disposal
You still could not make them vote with stomachs
Isinkwa and *impupu* could have worked
What about chicken pieces from nandos
Those were not there at your rallies
Why did you not even bus supporters to FNB
Those images did not show the numbers
Why did you not ask if they wanted short sleeves
Why not even ask if they wanted long sleeves
Look what you have done to our prestigious club
You have sounded the last post
You have fired that twenty-one gun salute
Now the upstarts are gaining traction
Look, they did so to *umdala* uKK
Now you let *amasimba* happen close to us
You are now a disgrace to liberation movements
How could you forget *umdala lo* uMkhonto We Sizwe

How slippery he was during the apartheid era
You forgot how he outwitted pipe smoking Mbeki
Madoda you are such a big let down lonke

Mantashe, Mbalula, Mashatile *lonke* you are finished

THE STENCH PART TWO

The putrefaction still here
The maggots writhing still
The stinking carrion there
Pungent smell in society nostrils
Like hogs wallowing in the mud
The braggarts show obscene wealth
Pungent, acrid, putrid exhibition
Incontrovertible evidence everywhere
Those diplomatic bags foul smelling
Customs officials turn a blind eye
Aiding and abetting the looting spree
The putrefaction there in the gold mafia
With no trace of shame they carry on
Our ways trampled under turd carrying boots
Villains and vermin are the new role models

Friends Or Fiends

Where I had sacred mountains
Today I have battered, barren plains
The rivers that once flowed fast
Giving life to abundant flora and fauna
Now deliver death to my door step
The mercury and cyanide contamination
What did I do to deserve this strangulation
So you call these putrid fiends your friends
The future is now destined for the morgue
The vile smash and grab right under our watch
British colonialism reduced to kindergarten stuff
Democracy in the workplace dealt a mortal blow
Those days of slavery alive and vicious still
The yellow slave master wields the whip now

Friendly Fire In Zimbabwe

There was Constable Chen
My wife had pummeled me
Sergeant Ai then walked in
In the company of Assistant Inspector Tao
Constable Chimumhu started that
When in Mandarin he translated

With my blue eye I went back to work
Mining manager Lei shouted at me
Human resources officer Bao was told
The paltry packet had a deduction
The hourly rate had to be used

The labour officer Jing sat there
His fellow labour officers were there
That was the caustic end of the matter
Summary dismissal was to follow

Souls For Sale

Peddling their souls
These mammon worshippers
Down on their bended knees
Exhibiting incessant begging
The mountains of shamelessness
Bowing and scrapping before him
That bulbous, humongous being
Oblivious of the price to be paid
Time to read the small print is near.

Statuette Silence

The streets are gripped
There is the statuette silence
The vociferation now a whimper
The ominous thudding of jackboots
Shattering that statuette silence

The mark of the beast seen
Seen there on their ugly faces
The hounds no longer needed
The black swine does its wicked dance
Lacerating flesh, breaking bones

The stylus still stuck on vinyl
The monotony creating melancholy
Inside our heads erupting thoughts
Erupting thoughts of rebellion
Thoughts presently bereft of evidence

The *Chitutes*

Jack Mapanje, that Malawian poet
Detained without charge or trial
Yes, by that demonic despot in Malawi
Compared them to that mouse with kleptomania
Chitute, amassing what it does not need

We have the *Chitutes* right here with us
By any means necessary amassing wealth
While the poor and needy drown in poverty
Their consciences long became liabilities

Their yellow friends leave us with nothing
Cattle, goats and sheep rot in the pits
Cyanide, mercury pollutes our wells, springs, rivers
Environmental management agents just look on
The castration of the nation long took place

What became of the real revolutionaries?
Where did these mercenaries sprout from
What is the source of this barren cloud
The barren cloud that does not bear rain
Where did this sense of entitlement come from

The Unthinkable

The kleptomaniacs at it
The gluttons among us
The unthinkable is here
Look around and you will see

They do not fret about it
Lip deep talk of sustainability
The granite hills becoming history
The undulating landscape gone

Someone tell Simon Chimbetu
That *boterekwa* is now gone
Tell that too to those Italians
Those Italian prisoners of war

The Great Dyke is being decimated
The ravenous search for lithium
For the exportation of platinum
Flattened for gold and other minerals

Where are you photographers
Where are you poets, singers
Produce those videos for posterity
The hills, mountains and rivers dying

The unthinkable is taking place
Those mountains will be gone
The hills are fast disappearing too
The rivers soon will not flow again

Listening

I long, long said it
The counterfeit story
Now you say it yourselves
Tell us what really happened
Stop lionising yourselves
To bolster your entitlement
To bolster your hyper-inflated egos
Yesterday we learnt of the downing
The downing of the helicopter
At the hands of the lone female guerilla
Then came the vilification over power
Later the narrative took an ugly twist
What do we now tell the nation
Now we hear there was just nothing
Nothing but that English erudition
And that refusal to wield the gun
What now did we tell the children
Are you going to do what is right
Get off your high horse and eat humble pie
The masses now wallowing in poverty
Those that bore the brunt of the war
Later to be sidelined by the mercenaries
Bob Marley had long seen it on the horizon
Those that bore the brunt remain quiet
Fear grips their minds as they are force marched
To listen to stale, crusty and insipid promises
While with impunity the opportunists loot
With the spin doctors now in overdrive
The new narrative is under hammer and tongs

The hare brained schemes we now know
It is upon us again that personality cult
Thought the lessons had fully been grasped
The same dog that bit us in the morning
That same dog bites us in the evening
What did we do to deserve such a dung heap

Anomie

Many sentencing themselves to death
Dangling, gnarled and knotted at noose ends
Others gulping copious amounts of rat kill
The few traces of hope fast dissipating
The chasms between the obscene wealth
And the stench of poverty in the shacks
Many now turning into codeine junkies
The factory sirens long fell silent
The ubiquitous hordes of the unemployed
Drowning in the murky rivers of illicit brews
Many turning to heinous crimes for survival
Many stabbed to death at illegal gaming houses
Many hoping for wins at mushrooming betting houses
Hear the wailing behind the prison walls of poverty

Where Are They?

Drowning not their sorrows
But themselves in cheap alcohol
At street corners gulping cough mixtures

Playing cat and mouse games
Shameless revenue collection seen
Municipal police and vendors battles

By the streams of raw sewage selling
Selling shrivelled fruits and vegetables
Vainly trying to evade grinding poverty

With wives and children bawling
Sinking into the darkest depths of low self esteem
Many are found dangling at noose ends

Terrible Twins

They were armed
Poverty beside desperation
They were an explosion
That was also an implosion

The rumbling of turmoil
Running in all directions
Everywhere smoke billowing
Then came calm after the storm

Daggers Sharpened

Those daggers now sharpened
There at the whetstone of negligence
The rising mountains of garbage
Many a town and city just an eyesore
The falling rain an obvious blessing
Turned into a curse by the uncaring
All kinds of flies multiplying like amoeba
The population explosion of the houseflies
The buzzing green bombers not outdone

Burial Ground

The myth of invincibility
Reduced to smithereens
The sycophants put to shame
For their talk of immortality
Born of woman he departed
Leaving empty shells at home
The multitudes without medical care
The sun then set in Singapore
That precedent was then set
The profligacy is put on display
Flying first class to seek treatment
Only to return as mortal cargo
That one shunned that acre for reasons
All that is wrapped in a vile veil of secrecy
The gullible are then bussed to the acre
Sending off the remains of another landlord
The propaganda machinery at full throttle
Spin doctors unleash tale upon warped tale
Tales of alleged consistency and persistence
Unwavering commitment to the sacred struggle
Of liberating the masses wallowing in neglect
Another narrative will then be spun again
History is indeed the tyrant's mistress

Gweru

Right on that plateau
Forlornly she now sits
Is this the city of progress
Now just another eyesore
The retrogression evident
Vendors line the slimy streets
A cacophony of voices is heard
Fierce competition for customers

Littered Road

The road is now littered
Bottles of cough syrup
Youth by the road side sit
Girls turn to nocturnal creatures
Parading their private wares
The hunt is on for the dollar

The road is now littered
With impunity laws broken
Law enforcers turn into robbers
Peddling the confiscated drugs
Immersed in human trafficking
Taking bribes without flinching

The road is now badly littered
When did we become drenched
No longer cherishing working
Queueing for those trinkets
Blind to those hidden costs
See the road is badly littered

Done And Dusted

Nothing remains here
The york is long gone
The egg white is gone
There just is no passion
Just going through the motions
Just for those peanuts
The mercenaries are here
It is just like prostitution
All bereft of emotional attachment
There is just all the clock watching
All day long pretending to be busy
Threadbare jackets run offices
Office bearers absent in all respects
False kings and queens of the earth
Their hyperinflated egos on display
Service delivery dealt a mortal blow
The maggots writhing in the rottenness

A Fool's Sordid Tale

A smile bright
Just like the rising sun
Birds of all plumage Twitter
The vipers are out there

With the paltry pay packet
Tucked out of robbers' sights
The rustic whistles in contentment
The foolishness has not left

Old schemes are new to him
In his mind's eye he sees it all
The pay packet multiplied ten fold
With the wife smiling from ear to ear

He then falls for the candy coated poison
The cocaine like addiction got him
The candy talk and desperation
The snare of quick riches got him

Sold Souls

Jostling for the trough
A place on the gravy train
Even those men of the cloth
At their mouths the froth
Yearning for the evil broth

Peddling their very souls
Singing for their supper
Blaspheming with no trace of fear
Devil worshippers turned into saints
Sycophants singing for pieces of silver

Yesterday propping that despot
Not a single lesson learnt then
A chance of getting redemption lost
Stroking those hyper-inflated egos
The mark of the beast plain to see

The Donkey

It did not end well
The bag of mealie-meal
The man blinded by rage
The boy covered in dust
The woman deep in agony

The donkey had had enough
Headed straight to the low branches
Low lying branches of the acacia tree
The man, the woman, the boy too
And the bag came tumbling down

What Happened?

What happened to all those workers
Riding on their cycle to Bata factory
Facing the early morning rising sun
Facing the setting sun to go make shoes

What happened to all those workers
Those that faced the heat at Zimcast
As they ladled into moulds, cast iron
Moulding all sizes of three legged pots

What happened to all those workers
Turning up for the numerous shifts
Alloying those metals at ZimAlloys
Braving those extremely high temperatures

What happened to all those workers
Working with those secret ingredients
Manufacturing the famous coca-cola drink
And everything else called by that name

What happened to all those workers
There at Zimglass moulding bottles
All kinds of bottles for all kinds of products
Weighing broken bottles brought by the poor

What happened to all those workers
Manufacturing all kinds of abrasives
There at the now dead and buried Caridorn
At that factory along Bristol road

What happened to all those workers
Then rushing to the factory gates
Rushing to the shrill of the factory sirens
There to sell their labour for survival
Tell me now what happened to them all

Symptoms

The naivety marches on
The refrain resonates
Declaring war on drugs
The root cause ignored

Clad in their pristine uniforms
With the drum majorettes
Criminals in disguise there too
The disguised hypocrisy

Blind to the hopelessness
Watching the jobs sold
Blinded by the gluttonous class
Blind to avarice and profligacy

The root cause plain to see
The panacea grimly ignored
A nation in the throes of death
The master class enjoying trinkets

Of Blindness And Darkness

That gross violation shelved
The primeval beast released
The venomous villain now feted
The victim is once more victimized
With her tormentor stealing the show
Her worst fears are not unfounded
The hyena is out to devour the goats

The lack of solidarity is on display
The humongous tails now wiggling
The overripe pawpaws now bobbing
Blind to the schemes of objectification
Minds won over by the dished trinkets
While that girl remains physically scarred
The girl forever remains mentally marred
While the blind dance in the darkness

Not A Justification

If you know only the bright side
Then you have never known it
Then you have never known the moon
That is just the way it is supposed to be

To Solomon, wisdom and wealth given
Blessed with those seven hundred wives
That was not all for concubines were there
Today we still adore Solomonic wisdom

The dozen children with multiple women
Today we still listen to the great songs
That Jamaican will never be forgotten
The billions still inspired by those lyrics

Caught between monogamy and polygamy
Caught between western and traditional ways
And they walked away faces shame filled
For none could back then cast the first rock

The Fairy Tale

That fairy tale will end
That is just something inevitable
As the sun rises in the east
So will it then set in the west
After you have exhibited your worst
The repulsive control freak trait
Add to it the emotional blackmail
The elasticity reaches breaking point
This pool of patience running dry
That thin line will soon be crossed
Those photographs will be erased
All that will be in the mind's trash can
You will be transformed into a memory
Those happy times will be a distant memory
No attachment can result from manipulation

Off The Hook

You let him get away
Getting away with murder
You cling to false pride
You conceal your bitterness
In self persecution you wallow
He will reap where he did not show

He frequents the best bars
With his concubines giggling
Ordering seas of cognac and whisky
Cuban cigars smouldering on ash trays
While you have platefuls of bitterness
Many more will be shoved your way

You growl and like a lioness attack
Perhaps it is my time to walk away
The same way he simply walked away
To go and enjoy those strip teases
To tuck money on panties of lap dancers
Some measure of gratitude will do

One Way Ticket

The pool of patience then ran dry
Then he got his things and left
It became better to live on the housetop
For the heat had become unbearable
The emotional assault was stoutly there
There like a stubborn blood sucking tick
Tranquility had become a rare visitor
He decided not take even a back pack
He then went, went with the setting sun
Vowed never to return with the rising sun
The children had been turned against him
The mother had painted a picture of monstrosity
Maybe he should have had a paternity test
There was nothing, nothing he could salvage
Only the shell remained for the york was gone
There was a tempered steel yoke around his neck
Following the setting sun he sought his liberty
He was the devil in the eyes of the saints
There was nothing, nothing to lose, having lost all

The Monstrosity

The storm is brewing
Thunder and lightning
The political expediency
The war mongers' games

The monstrosity of it is here
The monstrosity of tribal superiority
Inferiority clad in ill fitting borrowed robes
Diffuse this ticking time bomb.

Summing Up

Not yet uhuru
The white elite replaced
Not by a black elite
Zezuru hegemony centre stage
The Zezuru kicked out
Karanga dominance at play
The agitation long began

Their Ways

I cannot say all those letters
Some refer to transgender
Others to gays and lesbians
I have no time for all that
Lynch me if you will I stand firm
Got no time for no time for *chichimon* ways
Got no time for *bumboklaat buttybwoys*

Yesterday you preached monogamy
Vilified the ways of our ancestors
Today you go to mountain tops
There you preach about gay rights
All the junk about lesbianism
I have no time for those queer ways

Reflections

Then we were subjected
Marxist-Leninist thinking
There was that propaganda
That abandoned road to socialism
Then Tiny Roland was embraced

Now the workers are orphaned
Now wallowing in abject poverty
Left to fill stadia for hollow speeches
For putrid , empty election promises

The kleptomaniacs long took over
Riding in fast imported cars to speechify
Then to their mansions for their feasts
While the poor drown in seas of squalor

The Grave Digger

The thud of the pick
The scrapping of the shovel
The cawing of the crows
The cooing of the doves
That is his soul soothing music

Along among the graves
His thoughts torment him
Labouring for thankless souls
Moving mounds upon mounds
Daily reminded of our mortality

There behind their oak desks
In plush air conditioned offices
No thought about him at all
Vain attempts he makes
To hide behind cheap liquor

He still hopes to get that one day
That one day they will sit and listen
That those numerous please will not fall
That they will not fall on deaf ears
Still the loner digs for rich and poor.

The Nocturnal Announcement

Darkness set in
Hyenas laughed
Owls eerily hooted
Witches' broth ladled
The witching hour looming

As if on cue
A dry barren wind
'Creaked and roared
Like creatures of the pit'
A dry wind with no rain
The gods have spoken

The dark. Dank announcement
Could not be made in day time
There under the cloak of darkness
Dark, dank deeds in the dark.

Pyrrhus

It was to be a time of bliss
Expecting ear splitting ululation
Accompanied by men whistling
Huge pots brimful of food
Brewers show casing their best
The drums of frothy traditional beer

The village in a funereal mood
Grey clouds of uncertainty evident
The village in a deafening silence
The celebratory mood dampened
Shocking revelations do the rounds
The boy had altered his school report
Turning his ' E' grades into 'Bs'
A clear demonstration of a warped mind

The villagers dragged screaming and kicking
Cajoled into drinking and eating
The echoes of drumming heard everywhere
The dancers not in sync with the beats
Dancers bereft of any traces of passion
Grey clouds of uncertainty drifting
In the distance thunder rumbling
Streaks of lightning in the greyish sky.

Vultures

They now descend
The many vultures
The carrion is there
Over it vultures fight
They tear off chunks

The shame of it all
Lying with forked tongues
Just a brood of vipers
Their candy coated venom
There in the lifelessness

The lifelessness now a podium
Each one with their warped stories
'Sailing miles from reality'
Embarking on their ego trips
A sordid show put on display

Thought Police

The stinking toxicity
The misplaced empathy
The fake sympathy
The thought police at it
The shameless censors
The narrow mindedness
The myopic thinking shown
The toxic thought police
Unaccustomed to free thinking
Forgetting that a picture tells tales
Congregating in their dens
Some with the spokesman ways
The cheap politicking exhibited
Those mourning more than them
Mourning more than the bereaved
It is a whole heap of shallow thinking
The blinkers firmly in place
Salman Rushdie sentenced to death
Such is the level of thoughts caging

Saints

Where one sees a villain
Another sees a saint
That is the way of the world
Is it a question of the chameleon
Does death act like a sieve
Separating the chaff of villainy
Leaving us to extol the virtues
The vile villainy dies with death
And all we see are those saints
All we hear now is your side
All you just hear is just my side
But where lies that impartial arbiter

Weird World

Conspicuous by its absence
The warrant against that criminal
That war criminal Netanyahu
In the same mould with Blair and Bush
It is a wild, weird , warped world
A warped international morality
The selective application of justice
Palestine under relentless attack
The blatant display of military might
The Israel war machine unleashed
The indiscriminate extermination of Palestinians
Supported by that evil Anglo-Saxon scheme
The war mongers' bereft of a conscience

The Broth

Clad in their birthday suits
Chilling incantations heard
The hyenas eerily laugh
In the darkness owls hooting
Discernible are the broth ingredients
Human heads, torsos, limbs, blood
The witches and wizards stirring
The sizzling hot broth is stirred
The witches and wizards bellies growl
The salivation there in the darkness
Death and destruction season upon us.

Winter Be Gone

Tossing and turning in bed
Those seemingly endless nights
Only later to hear cocks crowing
Myriad chirping of the birds
This winter has been too long
Plants' growth has been stunted
Some trees long shed their leaves
To ward off the looming dehydration
I long for the softly falling rain
For the croaking of frogs in ponds
I long for the sprouting green grass
For the kaleidoscope of wild flowers
I long to see the bees on their errands
Those stinky errands my compatriot saw
This dreary winter has been too long
I yearn to see the back of this lifelessness
I long for the long hours of sweet sunshine

Forever Changing

The river of time flows
No dam can hold it
Statues are swept away
The bronze Stalin statue fell
Unimaginable in his reign
That reign of famine and terror

The imposing Rhodes statue fell
Succumbed to the students agitation
The vociferation has been heard
That grave will one day be gone
The defilement of that shrine gone
Not one can hold back the river of time

Let them day dream of their immortality
The rain bearing clouds gather
The inevitable storm is on the way
The praise singers will sing that old song
The old song of condemning the pay master
The denigration we have heard before
History has the uncanny ability to repeat itself

A New Morality

Tear your dictionary to shreds
Your thesaurus incinerate now
Here are the new philanthropists
Bearing their ill-gotten trinkets
Beggars without shame salivate
Philanthropists with confetti like trinkets
While mothers daily die in child birth
In shells of hospitals bereft of drugs
The worshippers of mammon drive
After those foolish grins before cameras
The ostentation along pockmarked roads
This is the age of a new morality

The End

Now you hog the limelight
Now a gladiator in the ring
Enjoy it for the end is nigh
Into the trash can of history

There is no pot of gold there
There at the end of the rainbow
Go where now they rest in peace
Those that claimed invincibility

When they are done with the sheath
They do not want to look at it again
That there is your looming demise
The rabid dog must be shot dead

You will rue the day of your birth
Go on enjoy your ill-gotten wealth
Take your dirty secrets to your grave
You are now a liability to your handlers

Recess

Now we go appease them
We go do our rituals
The cow bells are ringing
Drovers off to the in-laws
There to deliver lobola cattle

The punishment is yet to come
Punishment for that defilement
That unforgettable sacrilege
The spirits were then in recess
Now the courts are in session

Of Blips And Blunders

Juju call your compatriot to order
His discordant voice is nauseating
The SADC hymn book is wide open
So too is the AU hymn book
Let us keep quiet about the EU one
For then a tongue lashing will follow

Juju ask your compatriot what he sings for
Could it be a lithium or platinum mine
Perhaps the remaining diamonds in Chiadzwa
Or some virgin arable land
Whatis it that has stolen his eyesight
Spare the Boer Juju and shoot Mbaura

A brazier left overnight starved of oxygen
The generated carbon monoxide spells death
Our compatriots turned into crocodiles' food
Bludgeoned to death in Afrophobic attacks
Necklaced over spaza shops and other menial jobs
Juju tell Fikile Mbaula Mbalula *sesifikile eGoli*

Is it some myopic mindedness at play here
Yesterday saying our doctors work in restaurants
Today he wines and dines with primeval beasts
Look to the north and the trekking to Mzansi
Tell Mbalula *sesifikile manje* by hook or crook
It is the grim necessity that is prodding us

Just tell your compatriot to stick to his lane
That he may avert a looming disaster
Who has paid the piper for this discordant tune
Tell this Mbalula, Mbaura or whatever to zip up
The economic refugees yearn to be back home
Advise him to put his brain in gear first.

Saka Muchaita Sei (So what will you do?)

That statement brimming
Brimming with the arrogance
The arrogance of unfettered power
In the hands of those braggarts

Saka muchaita sei
When we take the gold
Take it all to Dubai
Taking diamonds to China
The lithium too siphoning
Flattening the granite hills

Saka muchaita sei
When we have our diplomatic bags
Immune to the searching rigmarole
And we take out anything
When we can even take you out

Saka muchaita sei
We are the invincible army
The ubiquitous intelligence services
The baton wielding pulverising police
When we are even the captured courts
Saka muchaita sei

Saka muchaita sei
Answer me now *muchaita sei*
Tinenge tichingotonga tichingotonga

Nzou ichingofamba imbwa dzichivukura
The elephant striding majestically
Saka muchaita sei

Saka muchaita sei
We leave you with holes in the ground
We fly abroad for treatment
You wait for death in those hospitals
A barren **indoctrination** for your graduates
Future workers for our children
Saka muchaita sei?

The Beginning Of The End

With logs in their ears
With newly found arrogance
They never listened at all
The prophets sounded warnings
The Ides of March foretold
The soothsayer was just trash

In the beginning was the end
The blue print was there all along
The lessons were there in the errors
History was replete with those lessons
They were draped in the myth of invincibility
The praise singers sounded the death knell

The ebbing tide of the arrogance of power
The beginning of the end is at hand
The raving and the ranting has begun
The drowning in the rivers of innocent blood
The blue print was the ignored compass
This impending ignominy could have been averted

The Patriots

They will shamelessly blip and blunder
Knaves myopic minds fully on display
Teaching us about undying love
That we should love our country
Love it just like how they do it
It was just about the wrong bag
For besmirching our angelic names
With imagined law suits we pounce
The lessons in patriotism galore
Fat swiss bank accounts for patriots
Fortified mansions at home and abroad
For the inevitable torrents may come down
Flying first class for world class health care
Patriots sending children to varsities overseas
We all will drink from the wells of patriotism
Never again to cast aspersions on patriots

The Influences

I write what I like
Am a student of Bantu Biko
I will speak of the wretched of the earth
For I learnt the lessons from Franz Fanon

Those lessons from Paulo Freire
Forever treasuring pedagogy of the oppressed

I will learn from Ernesto Che Guevara
An aspirant of international citizenship

I will walk in the shadow of Marcus Mosiah Garvey
Impugning all unjust and immoral laws with vehemence

Drawing from the lessons of Mqabuko Nyongolo Nkomo
I write this the story of my life

I will get a lesson or two from African luminaries
Among them John Magufuli and Thomas Sankara

Stolen

I was taken away
Away from Kariva
Away from Mutirikwi

Brought me to their great lakes
Taught me of Lake Huron
Eerie, Michigan, Ontario, Superior
I was taken from the savannah grasslands
Brought to the Tundra region
Took me to the prairies of Canada

They made me sing Baa baa black sheep
To justify their stinking greed
Grasped the rules of the game Monopoly

Then the cow jumped over the moon
And the dish ran away with the spoon
Sailing miles from harsh reality

Dry Pool

That pool of patience
Now running very dry
That harmless garden snake
Seldom biting, now bites
The purring domestic cat
Roars now like a lion

Pushed into a corner by poverty
The humble and the meek rebel
The days of poll tax stirred it
Have you heard of hut tax too
Marondera now takes the evil lead
All talk about the strangling bicycle tax

That pool of patience runs very dry
The seeds of hyacinth now sown
The thick mass engulfs the lake
The strangulation is now at hand
Are those the drums of war I hear

Quaking

The false brave faces
Spin doctors with tales
Tale tales full of nothing
They have jelly in the knees
Quaking in their boots
In the stranglehold of paranoia
Behind the gnarled and knotted silence
There lies the rising storm of resistance
The Wailing Souls aptly put it
"Kingdom rise and kingdom fall"
The tremor turns into an earthquake
The steel and concrete turns to rubble

Crumbs

Just those crumbs
That is all we need
Let them just fall
Fall from your tables
There where you feast
You the chosen few
It is not false modesty
Driven by need not greed
We know of your entitlement
You who fought all alone
You who were the fish and water
We are down on our bended knees
Begging for just the crumbs
That is all we are just asking for

Evil Inheritance

We will always remember
Remember that dream lost
That dream you trashed
The power hunger you exhibited
You were their evil mentor
Taught them lessons in tribalism
The weed seeds were there in the struggle
That vicious struggle within the struggle
With the regionalists masquerading
Masquerading as altruistic nationalists
A firm believer in tribal superiority
Today some say it is their turn
Their turn to just grab all they can
For they are the cream of the crop
The elite dogs guard their juicy bone
The feeding trough is theirs alone
Any other dog will be mauled

The Way It Is

The opulence exhibited
The lustrous oak tables
Sturdy teak desks there too
Clad in expensive suits
Giggling, smiling from ear to ear
And you think it is service delivery
It is about off road motor vehicles
To ride over all those potholes
It is about the latest Iphones and laptops
For technology is forever changing

Meanwhile the cat and mouse games
Municipal police at war with vendors
At times collecting revenue for nothing
The ever rising mountains of garbage
Cholera, dysentery, typhoid marking time
Rivers and rivulets of raw sewage flowing
Trinkets delivery takes the front seat
Service delivery there beneath mountains of trash
That is just the way it is.

Now

Yesterday in the trenches together
Hiding from those merciless vampires
Spreading death and destruction
Not dampening our determined spirits

Pursuing with that steely determination
Watering that tree of freedom with blood
Vowing never again to be subjugated
What is that unknown song you now sing

Who are those at the high table
There at the high table with you
There where no crumbs fall for poor Lazarus
Are those the investors with mega deals

With our chapped hands we raise the flag
With our dry mouths we sing the anthem
Our minds have erupting thoughts of rebellion
What ghoulish hand clamps our mouths

We see that endless banquet going on
The right words bereft of any action
Squalor there among us like a serial killer
The chandeliers will soon be smashed

Invoking Spirits

Rise you fallen freedom fighters
Rise to finish that righteous fight
Only half the story has been told
The struggle was long usurped
That so many were sacrificed for a few
That must make your spirits rise
Rise against the pseudo patriots
Those with that absurd claim
Claiming to be the only revolutionaries
Writing pages upon pages of warped tales
Giving us national anthem and flag independence
Their fiendish friends from the east just looting
Wining and dining with a select few
Arise now in avenging spirit form
Deliver the mortal blows to these charlatans
That blood that flowed at Chimoio, Nyadzonia
At Mkushi, Freedom camp and other places
That was never for the regionalistic schemes
And those dynastic tendencies now pursued
Rise fallen fighters for the nationalistic struggle

Tramp

The arrogance of power on display
That tramp strutting like a feudal lord
The verbal diarrhoea always spewed
The art of diplomacy never mastered
Calling other countries worthless shitholes
When it is his big mouth that is a sewer
That uncouth thug in that white house
There at the helm of the Ku Klux Klan
Trying to court the unapologetic Afrikaners
Sticking to their segregationist ways in Orania
That tramp strutting his stuff everywhere
That braggart on the fragile world stage
Hating with passion the people of Palestine
Bragging that some leaders lick his damn arse
That thug starting that tariff world war
That heavy weight bully flooring lightweights
Bringing the world to the brink of world war
The looming possibility of world war three
Just to entrench that stinking racial hegemony
Reducing SADC and AU to mere sand castles
Brothers driven to wield daggers against each other
Deep betrays leaving many countries in the lurch

Thick Mist

The moral compass long lost
Humongous women gyrating
Bulbous boobs and backsides
The sexually suggestive dancing
The objectification now complete
Hoping to draw that attention
Who knows what the prize is

The future in the throes of death
Death merchants without a care
Broncleer, crystal meth, mandrax
The nation on the precipice edge
The one eyed led by the stone blind
The nation lost in a thick mist

The ubiquitous stench of poverty
The crammed demonic conditions
No longer the house of hunger
But a half way house to the gate of hell
The many addicts in the gaming houses
Some to sleepless nights in flea laden hovels

The incessant, nauseous political bickering
The dog fights for seats at the high table
While hospitals become places of death
With schools going without teachers
When churches are brimful of charlatans

When kleptomaniacs become role models
With the poor licking lips in misplaced admiration

Many packing their bags and leaving in droves
To face the ever present xenophobic attacks
To go abroad and do funny things just to exist
The real possibilities of drowning in the Limpopo River
Many crushed by the jaws of the many crocodiles

The land of soiled, caustic milk and honey
That snot apple tree no longer bearing fruit
That barren cloud that bears not a rain drop
The fiery avenging spirit that we dragged home
The chocking ashes in the once blazing hearth
What is the source of the thick mist that will not go
The feast on the scabs continues with no end in sight

Pests

White locusts came
Descended in swarms
Blocked bright daylight
Thought it was a solar eclipse
They nibbled at the maize
A relentless war was waged
The locusts were annihilated

Now yellow locusts descend
Like Israeli jets from the sky
Bombing Gaza into oblivion
Yellow locusts spelling doom
Threatening the core of our being
That steely determination is here
Saving ourselves from extinction

The *Shitstem*

They promise dams
Where no rivers flow
It is the shitstem

Rivers of raw sewage
Cholera and cousins run root
It is the shitstem

Just those empty shells
With not even pain killers
It is the shitstem

After years of studying
Facing chocking unemployment
It is the shitstem

After years of hunger
You then vote with your stomach
It is the shitstem

You have long been blinded
You bash fellow sufferers
It is the shitstem

The poor in jail for petty crimes
The big fish tear the nets

It is the shitstem

So they keep us hungry
They appear like benefactors
It is the shitstem

The pock marked roads
They fly everywhere they go
It is the shitstem

The massive looting of resources
The stashing in Swiss banks
It is the shitstem

It is foul smelling
It is the system with shit
The shistem

Vhembe

Now called the Limpopo River
Let's tell the story of the river
That must be nourishing us
Nourishing the vaVhenda people
Now the source of gruesome deaths
Man eating crocodiles in the river
The wicked apartheid machinery
The wicked breeding of the man eaters
In vain trying to stop our liberation
The Zipra-Umkhonto We Sizwe operations
We still respect the colonial borders
The institutionalised foolishness still here
They tell us to forget who we really are
They tell us to forget who we really are
They commemorate their Vietnam heroes
They shed tears talking about the Holocaust
They say colonialism is a thing of the past
They say erase memories of that heinous crimes
The worst crime against the whole of humanity

In This Mind

What goes on in this mind
It is an explosion imploding
It is the volcanic eruptions
The hot lava of rebellion
No longer readable on the Richter scale
The mind shattering quaking of revolution
Walking down those sordid streets
The knives stuck in the backs of travellers
The ever bustling roadside flesh trade
Oblivious of the free flowing rivers of sewage
The ever rising mountains of dumped garbage
With service delivery giving way to privileges
When talk of revolution is side tracked by bed bugs
When potholes are filled with diversionary tales
The turbulence that goes on in this troubled mind
That is the implosion that is the explosion
Which could be the explosion that is implosive.

Slaves

"Kill I today you cannot kill I tomorrow"
In his booming voice the message carried
That young artist a vibrant new torch bearer
Years after his passing the message lives
Bob Marley still spreading messages of hope
The message of revolution here for generations
The baritone still carries the poignant messages
I hear Peter Tosh spreading that militancy still
"Till Africa and Africans are free"
They removed from the wrists and ankles
The chains are still there in many a mind

Then our people herded into the slave ships
Fellow Africans complicit in that disaster
Today the painful truth is in velvet cover
How long shall this criminal scheme continue
Nothing to show but those slave wages
Will that heroine's bones rise once more
The seer's road is laden with thistles and thorns
"Kill I today you cannot kill I tomorrow."

School Boys

Like school Boys they go to the office
That infamous office of humiliation
Summoned by the bullish headmaster
No, not the modern school head
The stern faced traditional headmaster
The exploitative Master in that nursery rhyme
There to be whipped with a rattan cane
There to be repeatedly verbally bombed
There to be taught good behaviour
There to be told who to arrest and trash
The carrot and stick method is used
The little school boys emerge chastised

Deep Chasms

Africa of deep Chasms
Wrought by those robbers
Those rapists around the table
There in Berlin, in germs many
Africa of the deferred dream
Africa embroiled in proxy wars
Waged to mask rampant looting
The founding fathers' dream lost
The present clinging to delusions
Loyal to ways alien to that dream
Anglophone, Francophone, Lusophone
The blind buffoonery bereft of direction
Complicit in the gruesome murder of Gaddafi
Putting Traore in those evil cross hairs
Rich Africa mired in abject squalor
Flying to beg in Europe and America
Africa of flags and anthems independence

Alms

Keep their stomachs empty
Hunger thunder always rumbling
Pluck the feathers of a live fowl
Embrace that stalinist thinking
Your boots' shadow is their refuge
Create that image of a benefactor
A god not lesser than the creator
Forever they should be grateful
Down on bended knees begging
Never. Never teach them to catch fish
Teach them to eke a living on alms
Retain power through empty stomachs
Keep them at loggerheads with urbanites
Those urbanites paying punitive taxes.

Vampire

There is the bloody vampire
Everywhere sucking blood
Tearing at the social fabric
We are lost in the thick jungle
In the jungle of lawlessness
Directionless with no compass
The moral compass long lost
The law now packaged and sold

Like planes on the runways
The buses fly on the narrow roads
Driven by those foul mouthed touts
Private vehicles not to be outdone
Law enforcers feign perilous blindness
Blinded by the rustling of dollar notes
Blinded by the jingling of coins
Rivers of blood flow on the roads
Ill equipped hospitals cannot cope
Broken limbs infested with gangrene
Hospitals bereft of basic painkillers.

Beggars

Begging bowls on laps
The solemn songs sung
The indifferent passersby
The dropping of a few coins
Into the rusty begging bowls
Asking for numerous blessings
For those hands that giveth

Hopping onto private jets
Landing in London, Paris
Landing in Beijing, Washington
Accompanied by large entourages
Putting the best foot forward
The opulent class of beggars
The alms are termed foreign aid
The begging carrying on still.

Nothing

We have nothing to show
When the truth is just said
The alluvial Chiadzwa diamonds
The unaccounted for billions
The ever present looting spree
In its wake the pungent poverty

Skewed

Now the poor have all the stolen riches
The rich have nothing but the scabs
That carving long took place in Berlin
Today we justify it as international law
Thinking it is an unassailable divine order
That keeps that evil umbilical cord intact
Siphoning our resources to the greedy west
To those that murdered the Arawak indians
To those that exterminated the Aborigines
The yellow man joining in the looting frenzy
Looting on a massive scale calling it deals
Cheered on by the clueless, craven overseer class
Still without shame driving Joseph into captivity
There is that allure of the ill-gotten demonic gains
From the calloused hands and broken backs of slaves
The slaves no longer ferried on the slave ships
Bruised, battered, humiliated at home by friends.

The Symbols

This is where we are marooned now
Pale shadows of our former selves
Wallowing in this directionlessness
Rapists are exalted and always feted
Basking in the sunshine of their villainy
Chanting nauseous slogans of sycophancy
Women with their mountainous posteriors
And over ripe pawpaw like milk gourds
Swaying them to lyrically empty, tasteless songs
Where slogans of death are always chanted
With those cars thrown all over like confetti
Diplomatic bags brimful with stolen riches
The gluttons are the new heroes and heroines
Those that supply no goods nor services at all
But still smile from ear to ear with fat accounts
Flying private jets to the world fashion capitals
There to brag about designer clothes and liquor
Trolleys filled with expensive bottles of whisky
These are the new symbols of our struggle
The purported men and women of gods galore
Drowning in the stinking Ill-gotten gains
Meritocracy was long dealt a mortal blow
It is no longer about what you know, not that
It is just about narrow perceptions of clans
The new symbols of our self determination
Maybe there is Chenhamo High in Beijing
The fangs of the recolonisation are plain to see

Feeding Trough Aspirant

Welcome to this elite cult
With fellow masked dancers
The oaths will now be taken
Crush your conscience now
Let it never nag you again
Crush it beyond recognition
Drown it in a hellish abyss
That you may lie, steal and kill
Let nothing stand in your way
The way to your place at the trough
Here where there are no multitudes
Embrace the feeding frenzy of piranhas
Drink human blood from human skulls
Drink human blood calling it wine
The mark of Cain on your forehead
Kill even your sisters to protect the cult
Pledge to destroy even your own mother
Roast your father for your place there
Nothing matters but the feeding trough
Promise dams where there no rivers
Bleach their brains with numerous promises
Eyes focused on your interests not friendships
Fully grasp the ideas Machiavelli spread
Walk on lest you turn into a mound of salt
Never will you unmask your fellow dancers

Baying For His Blood

The hounds unleashed
Now baying for his blood
A black General shoots to prominence
The house nigger on a mission
The master must be pleased
The nigger, the mouth piece of the boss
The pensive face of the black terrorist
That remains etched in our minds as we sing
"How long shall they kill our prophets?"

For daring to kick out the warped ideas
Severing that horse and rider relationship
Showing Macron, his old queen and others
Showing them the stiff middle finger
Sending the French back to their poor home
Their itchy fingers ready to pull the trigger
The neo-colonial hegemony challenged
Another prophet must forever be silenced

Ibrahim Traore the target of those assassin's
For daring to cast away the shackles and chains
For daring to challenge flag and anthem independence
Refusing to be a kitchen nigger feeding on crumbs
For refusing to give away three bags of wool
Refusing to be forever bound to those schemes
Diabolic schemes keeping Africa in perpetual debt
Masterminded by those evil Bretton Woods Institutes
The World Bully and International Ministry of Finance

"How long shall they kill our prophets?"
The cowards did not just stand look

Complicit in the murder of Muammar Gaddafi
The spineless men and women do not look on
Another prophet marked for a gruesome death
They may kill the messenger but never the message
The forerunners of our liberation live on
Not one evil man or woman can stop this emancipation train.

My Ant Voice

Drowning in that cacophony
Drowning in the murky water
The murky water of mind control
My ant voice now whimpering
Yearning to reach every nook
Yearning to get to every cranny
Delivering telling blows to propaganda
Obliterating those mercenary perceptions
Today there is that peddled entitlement
That untiy of purpose long dumped
History shown to be the tyrant's mistress
My ant voice rising, rising to a crescendo
Merging with other ant voices rising now
Voices rising from under mountains of lies

Triple K Man

It is there in your monstrous blood
That which informed the butchering
The butchering of the Red Indians
That which auctioned my people
Today you talk of imagined genocide
You have not uttered a single word of apology
On behalf of your genocidal ancestors
You have not given reparations for slavery
You profit from the turmoil in the DRC
You stand by Benjamin Netanyahu in Israel
While hailstorms of bombs pummel Gaza
You remain mum about the obvious war crimes
That genocide in Gaza you turn a blind eye to
You are blind to the gaping wounds in South Africa
There were the effects of apartheid are alive

You were long advised to blow your trumpet
To blow it there for there to be world peace
You blow it *ad nauseam* for your racist hegemony
You are on your ego trip causing havoc
Triple K man rid yourselves of those racist schemes
Blow now the trumpet of world peace and justice

Same Old Song

It is the same old song
The song of extreme agony
The singers have changed
So have the instrumentalists
The lyrics remain the same
The tempo has now changed
It is the song of unbridled looting
It is a song of those new footprints
Footprints of subjugation on the rocks
It is the song of Cecil John Rhodes
The song of David Deadstone and others
Today sung by new conquerors
Sung not in English but in Mandarin
Today we ask, tomorrow they will ask
What did we do to deserve this trashing
What did we do to deserve this thrashing
Mines, schools, places with Mandarin names
Show me Chenhamo school in Wuhan, China
Ming Chang primary school there in Shamva
Perhaps creating a new generation of workers
The proficiency in Mandarin coming soon
And then you ask: What's in a name? Really
And the blows of colonisation still delivered
It is a discordant, nauseating song of conquest
It is a song of certain death at the hands of friends

Mmap New African Poets Series

If you have enjoyed *The Stench*, consider these other fine books in the **Mmap New African Poets Series** from *Mwanaka Media and Publishing*:

I Threw a Star in a Wine Glass by Fethi Sassi
Best New African Poets 2017 Anthology by Tendai R Mwanaka and Daniel Da Purificacao
Logbook Written by a Drifter by Tendai Rinos Mwanaka
Mad Bob Republic: Bloodlines, Bile and a Crying Child by Tendai Rinos Mwanaka
Zimbolicious Poetry Vol 1 by Tendai R Mwanaka and Edward Dzonze
Zimbolicious Poetry Vol 2 by Tendai R Mwanaka and Edward Dzonze
Zimbolicious: An Anthology of Zimbabwean Literature and Arts, Vol 3 by Tendai Mwanaka
Under The Steel Yoke by Jabulani Mzinyathi
Fly in a Beehive by Thato Tshukudu
Bounding for Light by Richard Mbuthia
Sentiments by Jackson Matimba
Best New African Poets 2018 Anthology by Tendai R Mwanaka and Nsah Mala
Words That Matter by Gerry Sikazwe
The Ungendered by Delia Watterson
Ghetto Symphony by Mandla Mavolwane
Sky for a Foreign Bird by Fethi Sassi
A Portrait of Defiance by Tendai Rinos Mwanaka
Zimbolicious: An Anthology of Zimbabwean Literature and Arts, Vol 4 by Tendai Mwanaka and Jabulani Mzinyathi
When Escape Becomes the only Lover by Tendai R Mwanaka
وَيَسـهَرُ اللَّيلُ عَلَى شَـفَتي...وَالغَمَام by Fethi Sassi
A Letter to the President by Mbizo Chirasha

This is not a poem by Richard Inya
Pressed flowers by John Eppel
Righteous Indignation by Jabulani Mzinyathi:
Blooming Cactus by Mikateko Mbambo
Rhythm of Life by Olivia Ngozi Osouha
Travellers Gather Dust and Lust by Gabriel Awuah Mainoo
Chitungwiza Mushamukuru: An Anthology from Zimbabwe's Biggest Ghetto Town by Tendai Rinos Mwanaka
Zimbolicious: An Anthology of Zimbabwean Literature and Arts, Vol 5 by Tendai Mwanaka
Because Sadness is Beautiful? by Tanaka Chidora
Of Fresh Bloom and Smoke by Abigail George
Shades of Black by Edward Dzonze
Best New African Poets 2020 Anthology by Tendai Rinos Mwanaka, Lorna Telma Zita and Balddine Moussa
This Body is an Empty Vessel by Beaton Galafa
Between Places by Tendai Rinos Mwanaka
Best New African Poets 2021 Anthology by Tendai Rinos Mwanaka, Lorna Telma Zita and Balddine Moussa
Zimbolicious: An Anthology of Zimbabwean Literature and Arts, Vol 6 by Tendai Mwanaka and Chenjerai Mhondera
A Matter of Inclusion by Chad Norman
Keeping the Sun Secret by Mariel Awendit
سِجلٌ مَكتُوبٌ لتَائه by Tendai Rinos Mwanaka
Ghetto Blues by Tendai Rinos Mwanaka
Zimbolicious: An Anthology of Zimbabwean Literature and Arts, Vol 7 by Tendai Rinos Mwanaka and Tanaka Chidora
Best New African Poets 2022 Anthology by Tendai Rinos Mwanaka and Helder Simbad
Dark Lines of History by Sithembele Isaac Xhegwana
a sky is falling by Nica Cornell
Death of a Statue by Samuel Chuma

Along the way by Jabulani Mzinyathi
Strides of Hope by Tawanda Chigavazira
Young Galaxies by Abigail George
Coming of Age by Gift Sakirai
Mother's Kitchen and Other Places by Antreka. M. Tladi
Best New African Poets 2023 Anthology by Tendai Rinos Mwanaka, Helder Simbad and Gerald Mpesse
Zimbolicious Anthology Vol 8 by Tendai Rinos Mwanaka and Mathew T Chikono
Broken Maps by Riak Marial Riak
Formless by Raïs Neza Boneza
Of poets, gods, ghosts. Irritants and storytellers by Tendai Rinos Mwanaka
Ethiopian Aliens by Clersidia Nzorozwa
In The Inferno by Jabulani Mzinyathi
Who Told You To Be God by Mariel Awendit
Nobody Loves Me by Abigail
The Stories of Stories by Nkwazi Mhango
Nhorido by Siphosami Ndlovu and Tinashe Chikumbo
Best New African Poets 10th Anniversary: Selected English African Poets by Tendai Rinos Mwanaka
Best New African Poets 10th Anniversary: Interviews and Reviews of African Poets by Tendai Rinos Mwanaka
Best New African Poets 10th Anniversary: African Languages and Collaborations by   Tendai Rinos Mwanaka
ANTOLOGIA DOS MELHORES "NOVOS" POETAS AFRICANOS *10º Aniversário: Poetas Africanos Da Língua Portuguesa Selecionados* by Lorna Telma Zita and Tendai Rinos Mwanaka
ABRACADABRA, by Olivia Ngozi Osuoha
DES MEILLEURS "NOUVEAUX" POÈTES AFRICAINS *10ᵉ Anniversaire : Poètes africains d'expression française* by Geraldin Mpesse and Tendai Rinos Mwanaka
Taurai Amai by Cosmas Tasvika Manhanhanha
Nhemeramutupo by Oscar Gwiriri

Ntombentle: Selected Poems by Sithembele Isaac Xhegwana
African Poetry Anthology: Chapbooks, Vol 1 by Tendai Rinos Mwanaka, Lorna Telma Zita and Helder Simbad
Juices Of The Forbidden Fruit by Tapuwa Tremor, Mapaike
Like The Starry Night Sky, by Obinna Chilekezi

www.ingramcontent.com/pod-product-compliance
Lightning Source LLC
Chambersburg PA
CBHW071009160426
43193CB00012B/1980